T0332823

How to Apocalypse

An illustrated guide

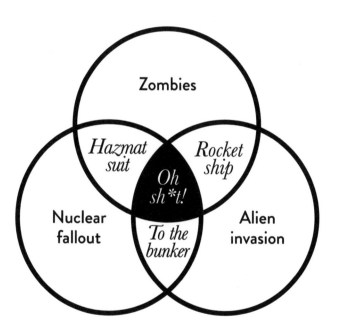

Stephen Wildish

Apocalypse ... now?

Contents

Introduction

Introduction

Picture the scene: the four-minute warning has been triggered, your phone is going haywire with goodbye messages and you're cowering under a mattress in your spare room. That's right – the apocalypse has begun and you are completely unprepared. You feel like a proper mug.

This book deals with how to prepare for all the wonderful types of apocalypses and various ways in which to attempt to survive them.

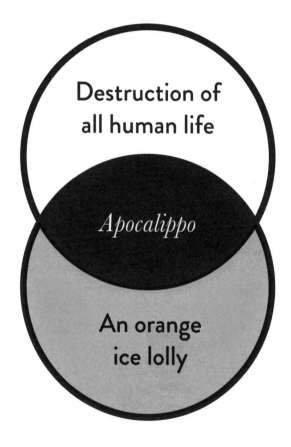

What is an apocalypse exactly?

In simple terms, the apocalypse is the complete final destruction of the world and with it all human life.

The apocalypse is a state in which civilisation as we know it will be completely fucked. Yes, *fucked,* that is what the top scientists use as a term for it.

It could happen overnight with the arrival of a giant asteroid, or as an awful accident when someone sits on the wrong control panel at Missile Command and butt-launches 400 intercontinental ballistic missiles, triggering a nuclear war. It could happen slowly with a particularly nasty virus or through climate change.

The basic crux of it is that everything and everyone we know and love will be obliterated, destroyed or consumed by zombies (depending on the type of apocalypse).

It's not all doom and gloom, of course; the apocalypse can be a really fun time for creative-thinking exercises like: 'Can I eat Grandma?', 'Can I fashion a weapon from a golf club and a bag of nails?', and 'Maybe I should kill Grandma first before eating her? But not with my new spiky-golf-club-killer-3000, I don't want to get it stained.'

Etymology

The word *apocalypse* has its roots in ancient Greek. It is derived from the Greek word *apokalypsis*, which means *revelation* or *unveiling*.

Most modern references to apocalypses come from the absolute maddest book of the Bible, which is really saying something: the Book of Revelation. The book describes a series of visions and prophecies about the end times and the ultimate triumph of good over evil.

The Book of Revelation is full of berserk descriptions of thrones encircled by rainbows, 24 crowned elders and four multi-winged creatures covered with eyes, with the faces of a lion, calf, man and eagle respectively. All coming to a head with the final judgement and the destruction of the world. Despite all the madness, it's still a better read than *The Da Vinci Code.*

Nowadays, the word *apocalypse* directly relates to cataclysmic events and the end of the world, usually with the word zombie or nuclear attached, and, in a frankly nighmarish scenario, both. We will never truly be prepared for nuclear zombies.

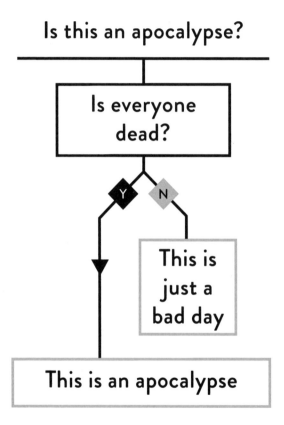

Is this an apocalypse?

Is everyone dead?

Y

N

This is just a bad day

This is an apocalypse

Past apocalypses

The threat of an apocalypse is nothing new. Humanity has survived, albeit only just, many near apocalypses in the past. Somehow we have managed to scrape through all this adversity so that teenagers can look at TikTok on their phones.

The bubonic plague

The plague, also called the Black Death, is a horrific bacterial infection that was on a mad European 'tour' from the 1300s, much like Elton John. But unlike Elton it ceased touring in around 1750 and has never promised that this is its last show.

At its peak the plague could kill 25 million people a year. If you were a lowly serf in the mid 1500s you would have died of, or known someone who had died from, the bubonic plague. Whole communities and villages were often wiped out.

The plague symptoms consisted of all the usual ailments: tiredness, delirium, headache and fever. So far so dull, but then comes the frankly uncontrollable violent diarrhoea, followed by weeping boils and blisters, coughing up blood and agonising buboes (massive black pustule-like swellings) in your groin and armpits.
No thank you.

Today, a simple course of antibiotics would clear it up before you even had to learn what a bubo was.

The Toba eruption

There have been a few volcanic eruptions that have brought humanity to the edge, but none more so than the eruption of the supervolcano Mount Toba, approximately 74,000 years ago. The eruption was the largest one in human history. There have been larger but we haven't been there to see it – something for the dinosaur version of this book to worry about. Although, imagining a T-Rex reading the dinosaur version of this book raises questions over how it would hold it with its little arms – maybe a smaller dinosaur would help turn the pages?

The eruption plunged Earth into a volcanic winter. A thick, choking blanket of dust and ash spewed into the Earth's atmosphere, causing the day to become night and making temperatures plummet as the sun was blocked out. Many a caveman's bank-holiday BBQ would have been absolutely ruined that year.

Plants, and in turn animals, would have died in their billions as the consequence of sun deprivation made its way up the food chain. The eruption decimated the worldwide human population from 3 million down to around 3,000. Quite the clear-out!

The Ice Age

Firstly, ignore the *Ice Age* movie franchise. Not because it's not relevant, but because they are all total shit. Anyone with kids will have been forced to watch that little prick of a rat or mouse or whatever with its stupid nut. Fuck that guy.

The Earth has seen many ice ages, where, due to variations in the atmosphere and the sun's output, ice and glaciers have grown and taken over most of the Earth for thousands, if not millions, of years. They have caused mass extinctions, obviously; you try to live in your fridge for a week and see if you survive!

The last ice age was around 115,000 to 10,000 years ago. Ice sheets covered the earth and the average global temperature was 10 degrees. The ending of this ice age killed off many species such as sabre-toothed tigers and mammoths. All species that if they were alive today, we would have probably blasted into extinction anyway with shotguns, so a lucky escape, perhaps?

Humans survived this ice age through a combination of fire-making, tool use and building shelters, but it was probably bloody miserable.

IT'S NOT THE END OF THE WORLD!

Optimists before the apocalypse

OK, IT IS THE END OF THE WORLD!

Optimists during the apocalypse

Assembling
your team

Assembling your team

Whatever the flavour of apocalypse you will need a team of people around you to help you survive. Selecting your team so there is no dead weight or rotten members can mean the difference between surviving and dying upside down in a car, on fire, underwater.

Now is not the time for niceties: if someone wants to join your gang and they bring nothing to the table, then cut them loose. Tell them there is a better group around the corner and run away. It's for their own good. Well, it's actually for your own good and that's all that really matters right now.

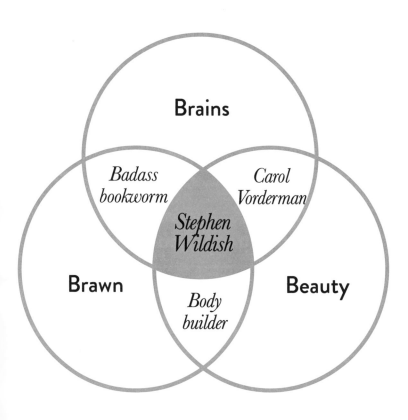

Which team member are you?

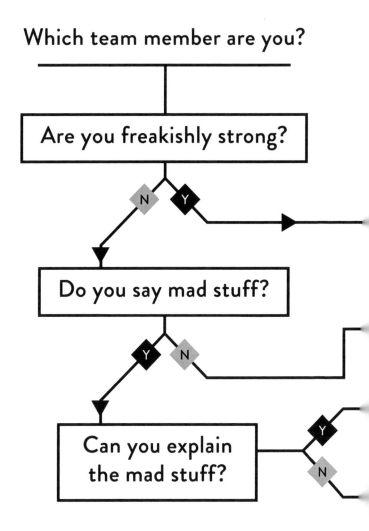

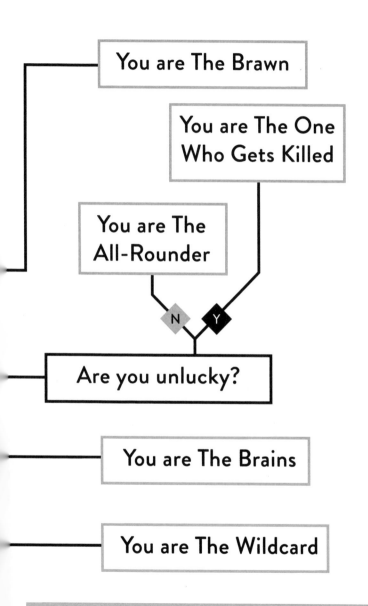

You are The Brawn

You are The One Who Gets Killed

You are The All-Rounder

N

Y

Are you unlucky?

You are The Brains

You are The Wildcard

The Brains

The first member of your team to find is The Brains. Your ideal candidate will have a working knowledge of science, botany, logic and medicine. All of which makes The Brains in your group an invaluable member. They can find a good cure for your headache, purify the water and solve cold fusion all before breakfast.

Because of their sheer weight of intelligence, The Brains will cause friction in the group, especially with The Brawn. Just make sure things don't come to blows; you don't want your source of knowledge regarding which mushrooms to eat knocked out cold.

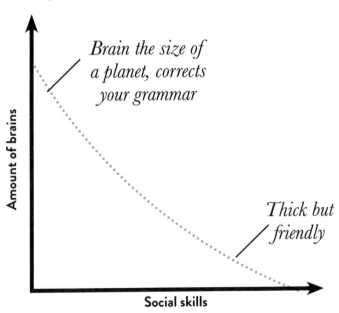

Brain the size of a planet, corrects your grammar

Thick but friendly

Amount of brains

Social skills

Strength

Intelligence

Common sense

Amiability

Likelihood of survival

The Brawn

They're as thick as a Boxing Day turd, but by God can they pick up heavy stuff. The Brawn is excellent at hitting things, killing things and smashing things. Think of the Hulk, but not green and wearing proper clothes.

They will have a decent working knowledge of rudimentary weapons, albeit constructed by hammering some nails into a baseball bat. They know how to cause some damage.

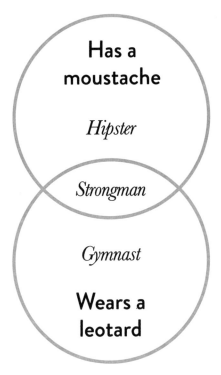

Strength

Intelligence

Common sense

Amiability

Likelihood of survival

The Wildcard

A crazed loon, good at problem-solving in their own special way. Can get into scrapes and generally behave like a dickhead, but it's worth it when one of their madcap plans pays off. Their highly different way of thinking will always mean they come up with a plan the rest of the team won't have thought of and it will either work out very well or very badly, but never anything in between.

Strength

Intelligence

Common sense

Amiability

Likelihood of survival

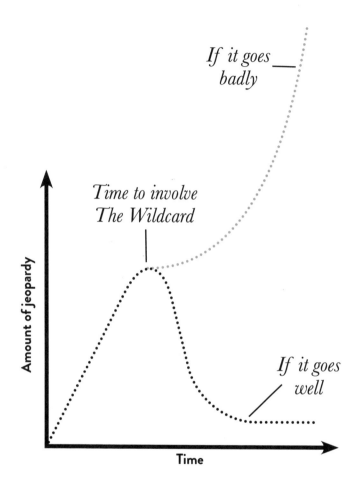

If it goes ___
badly

Time to involve
The Wildcard

Amount of jeopardy

If it goes
well

Time

It can be hard to put up with The Wildcard's many eccentricities and
The Brawn will definitely punch them directly in the face at some
point. It's best to stay out of that scuffle, as it won't end well.

The One Who Gets Killed

In a survival situation as dire as an apocalypse, the chances of one of your team dying along the way is great. Reduce the chance that this death is yours by recruiting into your team 'The One Who Gets Killed'. Then when he gets killed you can breathe a sigh of relief. Sure, you'll be sad for a bit but he is ultimately forgettable and expendable. Perfect.

To find your 'One Who Gets Killed', look out for a chap who seems to have no luck, someone for whom everything goes wrong. He will have had tragedies of his own, and will stare at a family portrait at times. Don't worry, it's all part of the story arc for when he does die.

It's highly important to find a candidate who is incredibly nice and polite. If he isn't, there is a chance that this candidate might turn out to be 'The One Who Double-Crosses You and Runs Off with the Food'. Which is a bloody nightmare; they still die but you lose all your food.

If you don't have a candidate for 'The One Who Gets Killed' then maybe it's you and it's really time to worry. Find a new team, pretty quickly!

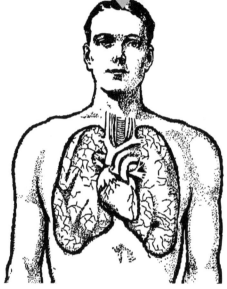

Strength

Intelligence

Common sense

Amiability

Likelihood of survival

The All-Rounder

The All-Rounder is pretty good at everything and probably a really nice person as well. Absolutely sickening, isn't it?

They won't be the strongest or the brainiest member but will have an above-average skill-set across the board. They will be able to support each member in their strongest skill. So if The Brawn needs help moving a tree or if The Brains needs help with a calculation, they can assist. Sometimes doing both at the same time.

Their one weakness is their underlying smugness, knowing that they can achieve anything. This was instilled in them at a young age by their model parents who nurtured every talent and had family meetings, like the Waltons or the Kennedy family from *Neighbours*.

In an ideal world you would be The All-Rounder, but knowing how rubbish you are at everything it isn't likely. You eat your dinner on your lap in front of the telly. This is not All-Rounder behaviour.

Strength

Intelligence

Common sense

Amiability

Likelihood of survival

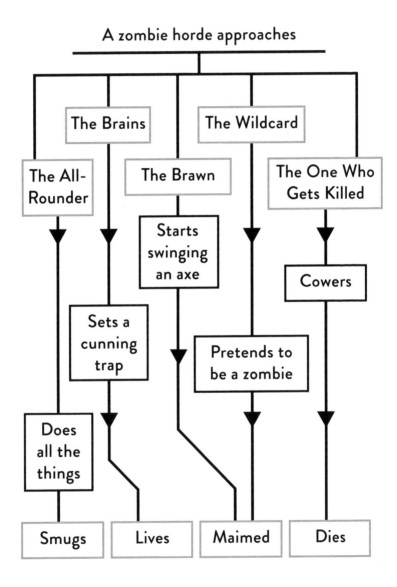

Team make-up

Making sure your team is well balanced is essential. You will rely mostly on The Brains and The Brawn to get things done and to generally survive. You can't have a team full of brawns and no brains and vice versa. A team full of brawns would be a meat-fest of brainless thugs, arm-wrestling and grunting and running into oncoming danger in a steroid-fuelled haze. Morons.

You would imagine a team of all-rounders would go swimmingly but all that smugness would quickly become too much to bear.

A team full of brains quickly gets way too nerdy and nothing gets done as they start to argue about the relative merits of various *Star Trek* series. We all know *The Next Generation* is the best one; move on, nerds.

Action time

OK, you have all your basic survival skills and you have your team prepared. Everyone is dying around you: it's time to work out what sort of apocalypse you are facing:

What type of apocalypse is this?

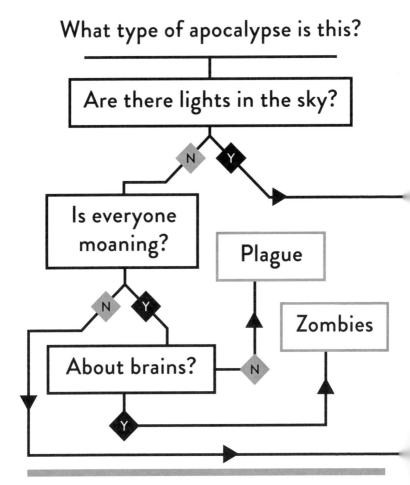

Are there lights in the sky?

Is everyone moaning?

Plague

Zombies

About brains?

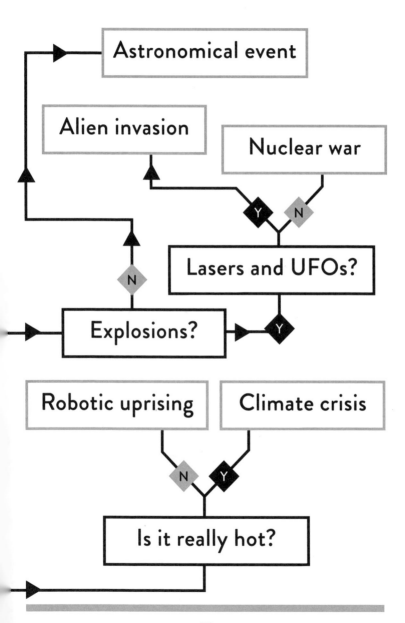

IT IS EASY TO BE BRAVE

FROM A SAFE DISTANCE

Aesop, stood behind his team with a pen in his hand

Basic survival skills

Basic survival skills

As the world burns around you, all the modern technology you rely on will start to fall apart and you will realise how poorly equipped you are to cope. Why does a kettle need Bluetooth, why?! Soon you will be left to your own devices to survive, so make sure those devices are not a broken fidget spinner and an iPad with 30 per cent battery.

Knowledge of basic survival skills in an apocalypse might be the difference between life and death, or at the very least making you look cool by starting a fire with some twigs.

**Day 45, you've started a fire but have no
one to show it to**

When to act and when not to act

To improve your chances of survival in an emergency
or possible apocalyptic situation, it is essential that you
act at just the right time.

If you act way too soon and go and live in the mountains
drinking your own piss, and the apocalypse doesn't happen,
well then you have just turned into a mad hermit for
no good reason.

Conversely, if you decide to act just after you are killed
in a swarm of zombies whilst you are sitting at home
watching telly, that is way too late as you are already dead
and dead people can't make any decisions at all.
Come on, this is basic stuff.

According to entirely made-up figures invented for this
book, seven out of ten people who die in emergency
situations fail to call 999 because they don't realise that
the situation they are in has tipped over into an
emergency one.

We tend not to want to cause a fuss and might just sit
in a burning building with our hair on fire before we
recognise it's time to act.

Surviving an emergency or apocalypse is all about
making the right decisions at the right time.

Take notice of things
Don't walk through life blindly: take notice of things that are happening around you, get off your phone. Is that bus heading right at you? Move!

Prepare
Think through what emergencies are possible for you in your current situation (i.e. don't prep for a tsunami in the Sahara). Make emergency plans and read excellent books about how to plan for apocalypses ...

Don't fear embarrassment
Standing out from the crowd and acting in the face of what you see as an emergency might feel embarrassing but won't feel quite so embarrassing when you are the only one who acted and therefore survived.

Where to start?

Focusing on your most immediate problem first can be tricky when the world is on fire and you've just experienced an apocalypse. To survive the oncoming weeks and months you will need to quickly identify your needs. If you are cold and wet, hypothermia is your immediate priority. If you are warm, focus on finding water as your priority: food and shelter will wait.

You can live...

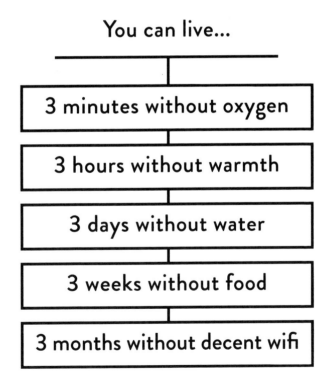

3 minutes without oxygen

3 hours without warmth

3 days without water

3 weeks without food

3 months without decent wifi

Anatomy of a Swiss Army knife

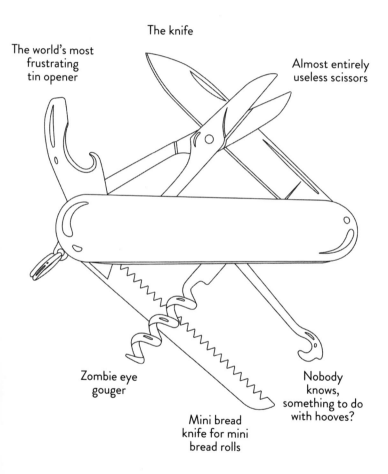

The knife

The world's most frustrating tin opener

Almost entirely useless scissors

Zombie eye gouger

Nobody knows, something to do with hooves?

Mini bread knife for mini bread rolls

Preparation

If you're reading this BEFORE the apocalypse, well done you. You're showing great initiative. Now is a good time to prepare a store cupboard of food in case the apocalypse does come.

You will want to store food that will keep well for years, so that means tinned, dried and vacuum-sealed foods. Make sure you store things that don't go off, but also things you like to eat and that have a wide variety of nutrients.

Method	Food	Use
Canned	Vegetables, beans, meats and soups	Student food sustains you
Dry	Oats, pasta, rice and flour	All the carbs!
Pickled	Sauerkraut, gherkins and onions	Fart fodder
Jars	Peanut butter, spices and herbs	At least try to make things taste good

Find somewhere to store your stockpile that is dark and cool, pest-proof and that no one knows about. Firstly so they don't steal it and secondly so that they don't take the piss out of you for being a conspiracy nut with 40 jars of sauerkraut in your cellar.

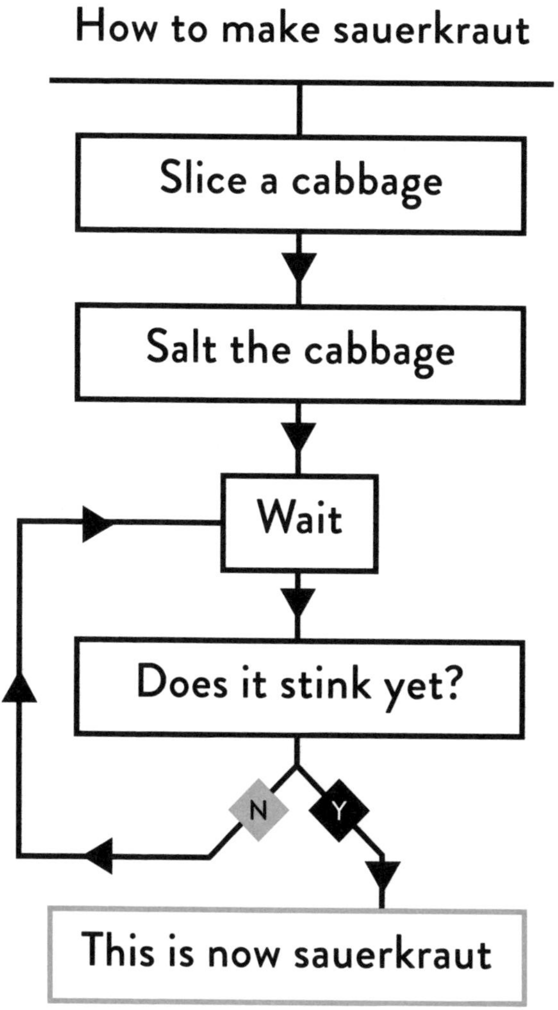

How to make sauerkraut

Slice a cabbage

↓

Salt the cabbage

↓

Wait

↓

Does it stink yet?

N → (loop back to Wait)

Y ↓

This is now sauerkraut

Survival kits

Having a basic survival kit stashed in the back of a wardrobe might feel like a mad thing to do when everything is fine but come the apocalypse it might be the thing that gives you the edge over the other plebs in the neighbourhood fighting for survival.

If you've ever tried to put up a shelf using the wrong tools then you will have experienced how badly a simple task can go for you, especially if you attempt it with a rolling pin and a paintbrush. So preparing a decent survival kit is all about having the right tools and knowing how to use them. The main features will be tools for cutting wood and starting fires, first aid for bleeding limbs and ways to treat and store water.

Make sure your survival kit is in a compact, small bag that is easy to grab and take with you ...

I knew bringing the air fryer was too much

Basic survival kit

Item	Description
Bottles	Much better than making cups out of leaves
Penknife	Never be short of tweezers and toothpicks
Candle	Turn all that alone time into 'me' time
First aid kit	Stopping you from bleeding to death
Mini fishing kit	Waste hours not catching anything at all
Whistle	To fruitlessly blow into the desolate wasteland
Mask	So you don't breathe dust, smoke or zombie virus
Torch	For seeing when it's dark, duh!
Plastic sheet	For making a shelter or a rain poncho
String	To tie your shelter or rain poncho
Matches	To burn your shelter or poncho when it leaks
Duct tape	Fixes everything on Earth
Wet wipes	Surviving doesn't have to mean sticky fingers!

Making a shelter

A shelter is imperative to your ongoing survival; it may be that you need a temporary shelter whilst you work on a permanent installation complete with running water. Years of sitting up at 2am watching YouTube videos of guys making swimming pools and two-tier hot-tubs out of mud and a suspiciously small stick are about to really pay off for you.

Preparing the right tools for your environment is also crucial. A good strong, sharp knife and a tarpaulin will see you in good stead for most eventualities.

Building a shelter with branches

If you've made it to some woods, then you have your building blocks for a shelter all around you. Find a decently flat area with a nearby tree that has split its trunk to form a nice Y shape.

Finding the flattest ground available will serve you well later on, especially at 3am when you are cursing the bumpy bloody rocks jabbing into your arse. Obviously avoid clifftops and the tops of hills; they might have great sunsets, but as Instagram will no longer be working the shots 'for the gram' will be a complete waste. High ground like this will be the windiest and most perilous place to set up your camp.

**Camping next door to the guy who
remembered to pack a saw and an axe**

Time to assemble

Find a long branch and put one end of it in the Y of the tree and
the other end on the ground, creating a triangle. Now start to lean
some carefully selected thick branches against your main branch,
acting like 'ribs'.

Time to test the shelter. First, test that it is sturdy enough, by gently
pressing down on the main branch to see how much it bends. If you
snap it now it will be annoying but not as annoying as testing it after you
finish. Second, test that it's big enough for you by lying inside the frame.
If it's too big it will be harder to keep warm in your shelter and if it is too
small then you're a fucking idiot who built a shelter too small.

Once you are happy with the shape and size of your shelter, begin
to layer up the sides with smaller sticks and larger leaves to create
some insulation. Plug any little gaps with leaves and moss. If you're
feeling plush lay out a decent bed of leaves, moss and pine needles
(if you have any) to make a soft, insulated floor. Check you haven't
also imported a billion bugs into your shelter with these materials or
you will be bitten to death by the little bastards.

Building a shelter with snow

Start by building a pile of snow as high as you can before your fingers
turn black. Pile it up in a rounded shape that will ensure that when it's
finished it won't collapse on you and entomb you in an icy coffin. Leave
the mound to refreeze, as this will make it much stronger. Maybe use
this time to contemplate all your terrible life choices that led you to this
point? Dig a small entrance hole and continue to crawl in and hollow out
the centre of the mound.

Can you build a snow shelter?

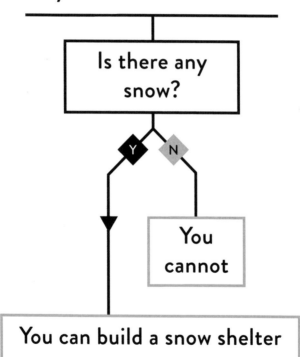

Is there any snow?

Y   N

You cannot

You can build a snow shelter

Fire!

You need to find logs, branches and twigs of many varying sizes, and a suitable tinder. Tinder is something that sets on fire easily even from a spark – it can be some dry leaves, cotton wool or any part of a shell suit from the 1980s (bloody lethal things).

When collecting your logs, avoid anything damp or mouldy as the resulting smoke from your fire will have you coughing like a chain smoker. Make sure you've collected enough large, dry logs to last you as long as you want the fire to burn for. You don't want to be stumbling around in the woods for more logs in the dark, muttering what a fool you've been.

Lighting the bloody thing

If you have a lighter or matches then well done you, have a medal. If you are unlucky enough not to have anything suitable then prepare for a couple of hours of swearing and muttering under your breath whilst huddled over some smouldering twigs.

If you have prepared a survival kit you can use the wire wool and nine-volt battery to create a spark by placing the two together. Though you have to ask yourself why you are packing these things and not a box of matches. Do you just like playing Action Man?

Rubbing two sticks together

If you are shit out of luck and have nothing to make a spark nor anything that will catch on fire from a spark then it's time to start rubbing sticks together to create a glowing ember. Of course this method won't work, but it will feel much better doing something rather than nothing, and at least you will be warmer after all the fannying around with sticks.

How to build your fire

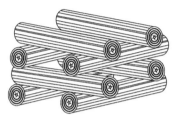

Oooh, someone went to Scouts!

The 'lean and hope' approach

The 'someone gave up' method

Water

Finding water in a survival situation is one of your first concerns, but making sure you don't give yourself cholera when you do find some is the next thing to think about.

Green vegetation

Following signs of green vegetation will often lead you to a good water source. If things are growing they must be getting water somehow. No promises, though: you might trek up a hill to find absolutely bugger all.

Rainwater

If appropriate (i.e. there is no nuclear fallout) then collect rainwater in upturned pots and containers. Try to keep these covered when it's not raining or you will be providing an ideal location for mosquitoes to breed and bite you to death.

Melt snow

If you have snow, then you can melt some in a pot. Crisp, white snow is a good clean source of water. Yellow snow is piss.

Trap condensation from plants

Wrap a sealed plastic bag around branches of trees and you will trap a decent mouthful of water over a day.

If you can't find a good source of water you might have to settle for a muddy puddle. If you've got a smug survival kit then you will have water purification tablets: bully for you. If not, then get used to the taste of potentially lethal water sieved through a sweaty sock.

Sieving water through a sweaty sock

Sieving water through a sweaty sock is the method of water purification at the bottom of the pile, but if it's all that is available then get peeling one off your cleanest foot. Adding in a dose of verruca or athlete's foot isn't going to help the flavour at all.

If you have any activated charcoal then place some in the toe of the sock. If not, you can put some ashes from a fire or some gravel to weigh it down. Pour the water through your sock, slowly – the slower the better. As you take a first sip, make sure you take a good look at yourself and what you have become. Disgusting.

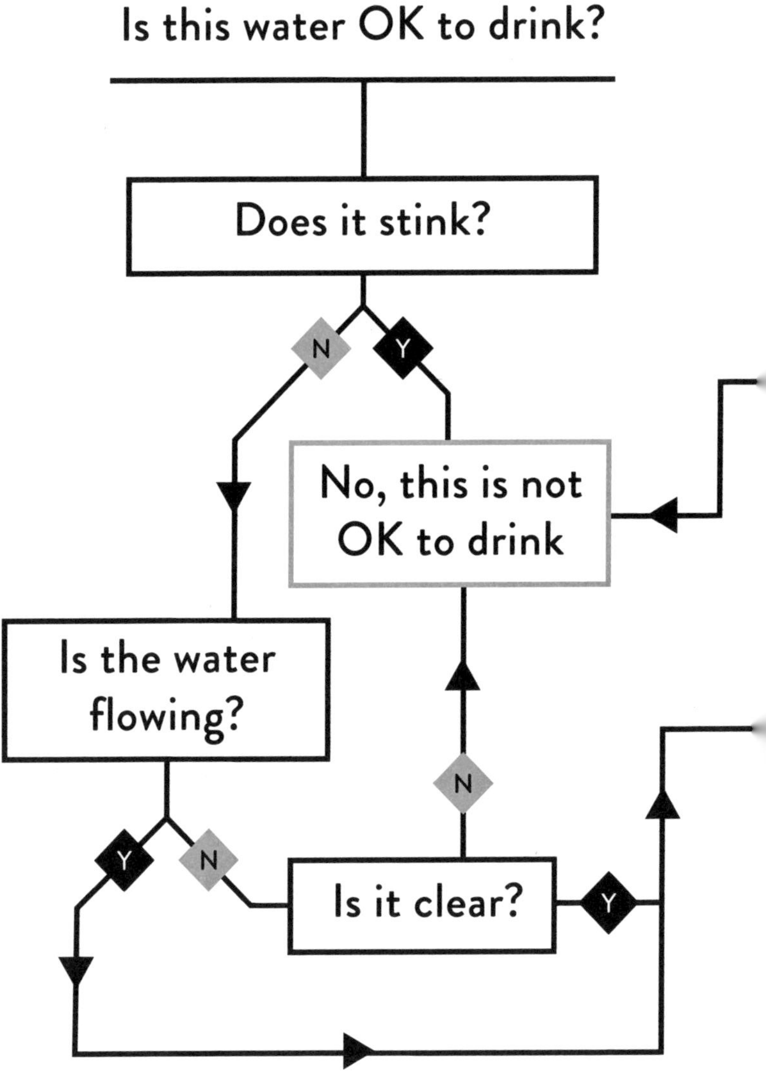

Is this water OK to drink?

Does it stink?

N　Y

No, this is not OK to drink

Is the water flowing?

Y　N

Is it clear?

N

Y

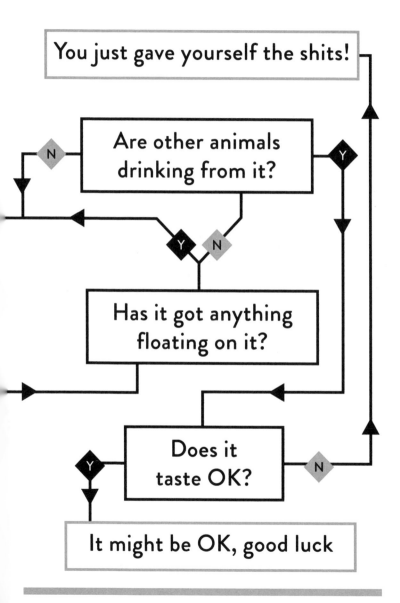

You just gave yourself the shits!

Are other animals drinking from it?

N

Y

Y

N

Has it got anything floating on it?

Does it taste OK?

Y

N

It might be OK, good luck

Foraging

With no one around, you can easily steal from supermarkets, but if you find yourself in the wilderness then a healthy knowledge of what food you can forage will serve you well here.

Mushrooms
An absolute minefield of delicious treats or poisonous delights that melt your internal organs. If you know what to look for then edible mushrooms can be plentiful and can sustain you for a decent amount of time, unless they kill you of course.

Hunting
As if you can hunt and kill anything! Give this bloody dream up now. Say you find a little baby lamb, could you throttle it to death? No, of course not. Go back to mushrooms and berries.

Plants
There are plenty of edible plants out there, from wild garlic to nettles. Just don't get your mugwort mixed up with your deadly nightshade unless you enjoy dicing with death.

Growing shit in shit

If you're running low on good food sources, you can look at growing your own. The two 'toes' are a good place to start: potatoes and tomatoes.

Potatoes contain all the essential amino acids you need to build proteins, repair cells and fight diseases. Unfortunately if you just ate potatoes you would eventually get vitamin and mineral deficiencies and die of scurvy like an 18th-century pirate. So you want to also grow some tomatoes. Equipped with these two plants you can make all sorts of recipes like tomatoey potatoes and potatoey tomatoes. Delicious.

To grow a potato all you need is an old potato that has started sprouting. Just dig a hole and put it in the ground. You can use your own shit as fertiliser. If you really want?

To grow tomatoes find yourself an old yoghurt pot or similar, fill it with mud (not shit) and put your tomato seed on top. Water it well, cover with a plastic bag and leave somewhere warm to germinate. Once it has sprouted and is a decent size you can transfer it to a larger pile of mud (mixed with your shit if you're now into it) and wait until everything is ripe to harvest.

Your crops will need watering regularly which you can probably do with your own piss. Sure, why not? You seem to be all about that now. These cursed potatoes had better be worth it.

Cooking

If you have the luxury of food, water and fire in your survival situation, then you might begin to wonder how to cook the food. It's unlikely that you will have access to your full set of Le Creuset copper-bottom pans, so you will need some solutions to help you whisk up that questionable mushroom you've been looking forward to all day.

Stone boiling

If you only have plastic containers for water you can heat up some stones in the fire and pop them into the water filled container to get it boiled. Pop in your food to heat to the delightful 'luke-warm' temperature that just about makes your meal edible. Mmmm!

Plank cooking

Use a flat piece of wood to cook your food on, positioned directly over the fire. Soak the plank in water to make it last longer before it goes up in flames as well. Ideally if you can find a piece of polished oak it will look beautiful. So as well as cooking the food you can pretend you're on a posh cooking show. Perhaps talk to a pretend camera whilst you cook?

Wrapping in leaves

The biggest challenge in wrapping your food in leaves to cook is finding non-toxic leaves. There are plenty of evil ones around for you to poison yourself with! Try to find wild garlic or horseradish leaves and, if you have gloves, nettles.

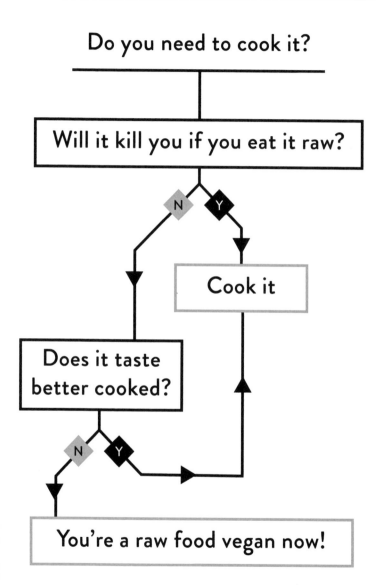

Do you need to cook it?

Will it kill you if you eat it raw?

N Y

Cook it

Does it taste better cooked?

N Y

You're a raw food vegan now!

First aid

Familiarise yourself with your first aid kit (if you are smart enough to have one). Now your arm is hanging off and you're pissing blood, that tiny bandage and plaster is going to REALLY help!

As the apocalypse has just happened, you will be experiencing a certain amount of shock. If the 1950s are to believed, a cup of sweet tea will cure shock, but then they also believed that a cup of tea cures your arm hanging off. It doesn't.

If you need first aid it's important to keep warm and lying down. Try not to move around too much until you have worked out how badly messed up you are.

Your initial priority is to stop any bleeding. First, elevate the wounded area and apply pressure using a cloth (clean obviously, you don't want to use a dirty old rag), dried seaweed or moss.

If you can't stop the bleeding, tie a belt, rope or similar between the injury and the heart to make a tourniquet. If you manage to stop the bleeding, make sure to wash and disinfect the wound. If you don't manage to stop the bleeding, well that's the end of you. Bon voyage!

Hygiene

It might feel a bit weird to be thinking about good hygiene at a time like this, but even in this apocalyptic world bacteria, infections and parasites still exist. You still need to practise good hygiene where possible around food and open wounds. The last thing you need is to develop an infection, gangrene or more likely a decent case of the shits. Squatting in a desolate wasteland shitting your life out of your arse isn't going to do a lot for your morale.

Wash your hands in water that's as clean as you can find, scrub under your fingernails and rinse your face. If you don't have any soap you can heat some water up and add pine cones to make an infusion. The pine cones have antiseptic properties, probably? Cool this infusion down a little and use it to wash with. Don't pour boiling water on your hands: yes they will be sanitised but they will also be burnt to shit.

No matter how tempted you are, none of this collection should be stuck up your arse

Toilet paper

Now that society has gone to shit you can use any bit of paper you like to wipe your bum with. Why not have fun with it and use an important legal document or a £20 note.

If you're in the great outdoors then you can use carefully selected leaves. Try one out first on your arm or elbow to see if you react badly. If you do choose a nettle or something too fibrous you will inflame your nipsy and will need to take steps to prepare a balm for it. Look at the actual state you've got yourself in, you're a mess.

To make a skin balm, infuse any oil you have to hand with lavender, pine and honey. Be very careful to strain it before use; nobody needs a pine needle stuck up their chuff.

Another way to keep your bum squeaky clean is to use a damp sponge on a stick. For god's sake wash it after every use.

Should I wipe my arse with it?

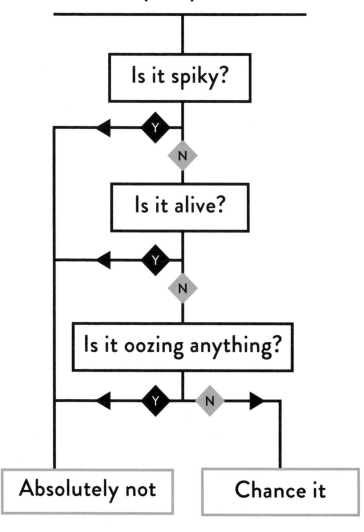

EVERYONE IS MAKING APOCALYPSE JOKES

LIKE THERE IS NO TOMORROW

A top-level Dad joke

Total nuclear war

Total nuclear war

Mankind's worst fears have been realised: the world's barmiest leaders have finally done it. They've launched nuclear warheads, thousands of them, at each other. Probably over a petty feud on social media. Now every country in the world is getting dragged into it by default, as the strike triggers an agreement that we all have to launch deadly missiles at each other, because if one of us has to have an apocalypse, we all have to, right?

When the nuclear missiles land they will inevitably kill millions, possibly billions of people and pollute the earth with radioactive fallout for thousands of years. Wonderful!

Boom

Making a bunker

If you are good with your hands and have a big enough garden you can build your own nuclear bunker that will protect you both from the initial blast and also the radioactive fallout.

Build underground

Compacted mud and soil is great protection so the best option is to build underground. This will also stop you from looking like a complete nut-job with a nuclear bunker in their garden because you can stick a flowerbed on top of it.

Digging down to a depth of around two metres will protect you, but also it's not so deep that if it collapses you can't be dug out easily. Use concrete blocks to build up the walls and make a decently strong roof from steel and cement. If you really want to go extra you can buy an old shipping container and bury this in your garden. This will give you a nice easy way to ensure the structural integrity of your build. So you can sleep well at night rather than staring up at your perilously flimsy roof made from breeze blocks and gaffer tape.

Emergency exit

Even if you are a champion builder with awards and trophies, you should build two exits to your bunker. The risk of being blocked inside by falling debris is great. If you do get stuck inside, you haven't built a bunker, you've just built yourself a miserable tomb.

Leaving this big hole in it was a huge bloody mistake

Is it safe to leave the bunker?

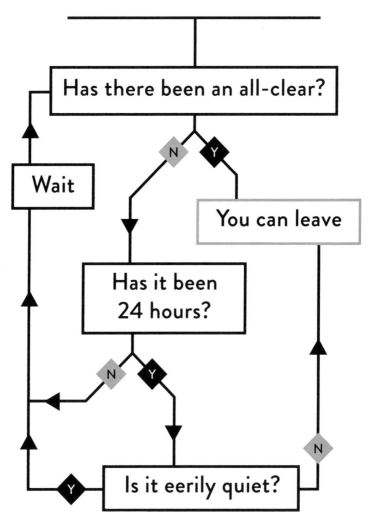

Plan to stay for two weeks
Once you have built your bunker, you can start to fill it with home luxuries, as you should plan to stay in the bunker up to two weeks. This is a good amount of time to let the dust settle (literally) and for radiation to drop to a decent level. Within that time the radiation should drop to around 1 per cent of what it was just after the blast.

You can't see radiation so it's best to stay in your bunker until you have been given the all-clear from a trusted source, not your neighbour Dave. He doesn't know shit.

Include a toilet
As you shut the door on your bunker and prepare for your two weeks of solitary the last thing you want to do is only now think about how you are going to go to the loo. At the bare minimum you want a bucket with a lid, but a composting toilet will be ideal. A composting toilet is just a big bucket with a lid and some mud in.

Prepare above ground
You do not want to survive for two weeks unscathed and emerge from your bunker only to be killed by a raging inferno of patio furniture outside the door. Clear anything away from your door that might be ignited by the blast beforehand.

Where to live

Bugger off!

To avoid a nuclear blast, not being in the country where the nukes are happening is a really good idea. Countries like Australia, New Zealand, Iceland, Solomon Islands and Vanuatu are the island nations most likely to avoid all this nasty bother, so if you can, live there.

If you are not prepared to up sticks and move to Vanuatu then you can find places in your country that are low-risk areas to live.

Don't live in a city
Cities are high-value targets as they contain all the infrastructure, financial centres and government buildings.

Don't live near a military camp or airfield
These are top of the list for annihilation as a pre-emptive strike.

Don't live near a nuclear storage depot
Fuck knows where these are, could be anywhere really.

Taking all this into account, the best place to live to avoid a nuclear attack is in the arse-end of nowhere.

Four-minute warning!

If a nuclear attack is on its way, it's possible that the government will send out a four-minute warning via text message. If your phone isn't charged that day then it sucks to be you.

If you do get the warning then get inside the nearest, strongest building. Your shed isn't going to survive the blast, but if you do want to wait out your final few minutes amongst the lawn mower and half-empty paint tins that is up to you. Whilst inside, move away from any windows and cower under a sturdy table. A nice oak table with extenders should do it. You wouldn't want to be fried to death under an Ikea MDF monstrosity, would you?

If you live in a city there may well be a designated nuclear shelter near you that would be worth finding out about before now. Hey, maybe you can go back in time and tell 'past you' all about it. No, you can't, you're stuck with this table in your back room.

Fallout? Boy oh boy!

If you manage to survive the blast then you will have around ten minutes before radioactive fallout arrives. The longer you can stay inside with windows and doors shut the better, as this fallout will be what kills you next after the initial blast.

The fallout comes in the form of clouds of dust and smoke, so now is the time to break out that super-duper mask you bought at the start of lockdown 2020 with the FFP1 rating. They laughed at you in the queue for toilet roll at the time, but who is laughing now? Well, probably nobody to be honest, there has just been a nuclear attack. If you are laughing then you're a bloody sociopath.

You are far safer from fallout inside a building, preferably lovely thick concrete without windows or doors, i.e. an underground parking garage, but the prices in those places will make your eyes water more than the bomb that's just gone off. Daylight robbery.

If you have to venture outside, wear clothes that cover your skin and dispose of them immediately when you return inside. Don't bring inside anything that has been outside and exposed to fallout or you might as well be outside.

Blast zone

A large part of surviving a nuclear strike is being in the right place at the right time. If you find yourself anywhere from ground zero to a one-mile radius with a typical nuclear weapon then you're fucked. Being this close is completely un-survivable without an absolute bloody miracle. The further out you get the less damage you will sustain but being miles away will be ideal.

It's not just the initial blast wave and extreme heat that might kill you: at ground zero there will be very high radiation levels making it a deadly zone to try to enter to rescue people. The rubble and collapsed buildings in the streets would be piled high and completely unrecognisable, making navigating around impossible.

Even the 'light damage zone' at around three miles from the blast wouldn't be a pleasant place to be. The pressure wave would knock your windows out and cover you in shards of glass travelling at vast speeds. Hardly a lucky escape.

A WORLD WITHOUT NUCLEAR WEAPONS WOULD BE LESS STABLE

AND MORE DANGEROUS FOR ALL OF US

'Mad' Maggie Thatcher

Zombies and
the undead

Zombies and the undead

Zombies don't care if you believe in zombies or not. They just care about eating brains and tearing your arms off and pulling your guts out. When the inevitable zombie awakening happens you need to know the rules of the game.

The lore of zombies has changed over the years as we learn more about them. Can they run or are they bound to walk slowly behind Michael Jackson? Will a silver bullet kill them or is that werewolves?

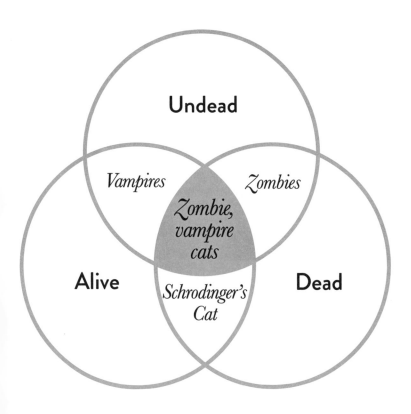

What is a zombie?

A zombie is a mythological undead corporeal revenant created through the reanimation of a corpse, or in layman's terms it's a dead person who is walking but shouldn't be. As unrealistic as a dead person walking is, there are three types of possibilities for zombies:

Biological zombies

Ophiocordyceps unilateralis, also known as 'zombie-ant fungus', is a parasite that infects ants, taking over their brain and controlling their body. It compels the ant to gain as much height as possible before causing them to remain in that position until the *Cordyceps* has released its spores. The process drains its host completely of nutrients and kills them. All pretty terrifying. It's not beyond the realm of possibility that a variant of *Cordyceps* could evolve that could control the human brain. It might even evolve to help you make better decisions than you make now. Maybe it would be a better person than you.

This is not one of the two things it looks like!

Killing your first zombie can be tricky to explain

Ghost zombies

This is the far-fetched possibility, in which ghosts (that obviously don't exist), or another sort of supernatural power have somehow caused the dead to rise. In this scenario, long-dead skeletons are somehow able to walk, without muscles ligaments or flesh.

Have you ever tried to walk with merely a sprained ankle? Yes, impossible. Now try to imagine doing this with only bones and a draping of mouldy skin. You can tick this off the list of things that won't happen now.

Chemical zombies

If you have walked through town centre on a late Saturday night then you'll have seen people off their nut on cake, or foghorn leghorns or whatever people call drugs these days. They will be stumbling around brainlessly, emitting foul smells and effluent into the streets and generally being a danger to themselves and to you. Well, that's what a chemical zombie is.

A chemical ingested either purposefully or accidentally that completely alters human behaviour either in the short term or long term would be dangerous enough to cause a zombie apocalypse. It could be a cloud of gas that a Bond villain has released for nefarious reasons. But knowing human nature, it's more likely to be released from a chemical factory by accident because someone pressed the wrong button.

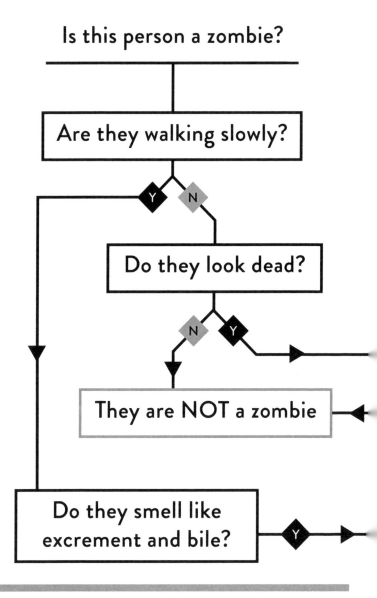

Is this person a zombie?

Are they walking slowly?

Y N

Do they look dead?

N Y

They are NOT a zombie

Do they smell like excrement and bile?

Y

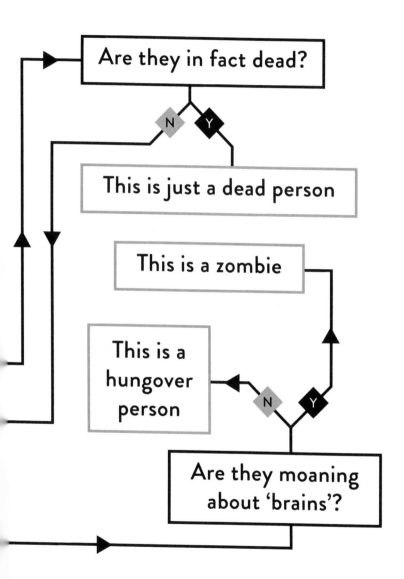

Are they in fact dead?

N — Y

This is just a dead person

This is a zombie

This is a hungover person

N — Y

Are they moaning about 'brains'?

How to kill zombies

Most zombies can be stopped the same way you stop a normal alive person, by chopping off or destroying their head. If you've ever tried to chop someone's head off then you probably need to stop reading this and go and hand yourself into a police station. Seriously, that's not OK. But if you have, you will know that it is hard to do.

The flesh and muscles of zombies are a lot easier to damage. They're not getting the correct nutrition or sleep to keep everything supple. Have you ever seen a zombie doing some warm-up stretches or yoga? No. They would probably break. Because of this, your weaponry doesn't have to be professional and can be much more improvised. If you don't have access to an Uzi 9mm, or a pump-action shotgun, then a good screwdriver, bread knife or rolling pin will do fine. If you are facing a decent 'horde' of zombies then an upturned lawnmower should make good short work of them. Just try not to slip on the blood.

Wait it out

Despite being undead, zombies still obey the laws of physics and thermodynamics, so if you wait it out long enough in your zombie shelter, they will die from malnutrition. Make sure you wait long enough for them all to be definitely dead. If you leave too soon and there is just one left then you fucked up. An estimate would be six months in hiding to ensure that the initial infected zombies and the secondary infected are all dead, but who is to say how long to wait it out in this entirely ludicrous and frankly made-up situation.

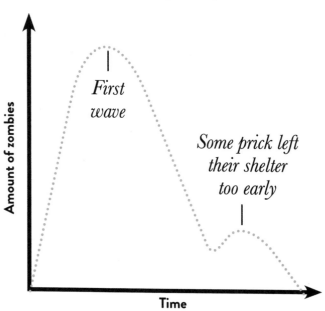

Zombie bites

Zombies make you a zombie with a simple bite. It's like multi-level marketing schemes but with more brains involved.

Depending on the severity of the bite it might kill you quickly or take a few days to kick in. After the bite kills you, you'll come back and kill the others in your group. It's a bloody nightmare.

There is a theory that if you get bitten on an extremity you can 'simply' chop your arm off and not turn into a zombie yourself. If you've ever tried to perform home surgery on a nasty splinter you will know how hard it is to even think about cutting your skin never mind hacking through your own muscle and sinew, all one-handed!

If you did manage to hack your arm off, without access to proper medical care you'll either die from blood loss or die from a secondary infection. Dying not from a violent zombie ripping you apart but from sepsis is the dull side of the zombie apocalypse they don't tell you about in the movies.

If someone in your group goes all quiet and moody (looking to 'The One Who Gets Killed' as the main culprit) then it's time to start checking arms and legs for bites and get hacking!

Zombie-proof outfits

Considering a zombie's passion for brains, an effective zombie-proof outfit should start with the helmet. Use something tough that offers maximum visibility.

A leather jacket is functional and tough, and also makes you look really cool when twinned with a pair of sunglasses. But for maximum protection, consider raiding a museum or your local National Trust property for a suit of armour. Good luck biting through that, you flesh-stripped dickheads.

Finding a safe zone

As your zombie-fighting team moves around trying to stay alive, you will inevitably begin to dream of finding a safe zone. A space that is protected from the zombies. With working amenities and sustenance. If you could only find it you might be able to get a decent night's sleep and a bubble bath to wash some of the zombie blood off.

Military bases

Unless they have been overrun, a military base is a good place to start on your search for a safe zone. The base will have natural defences, a fenced-off perimeter and weapons, many weapons! Your first challenge will be not getting shot by the inhabitants as you approach the base. Use a white flag or something to show that you're not in fact a zombie.

The mountains

The hardy terrain of the mountains makes an excellent safe zone. It's also a tranquil, beautiful environment to try to forget all of the awful things you've just seen.

Zombies can't swim, can they? Surely not?

Should you search for a safe zone?

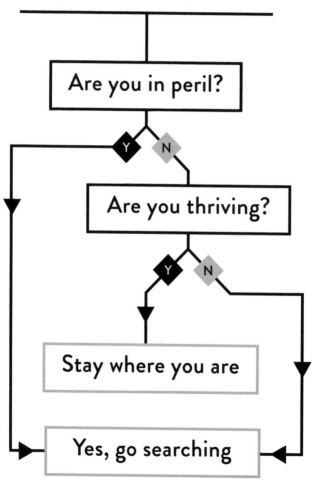

Are you in peril?

Y   N

Are you thriving?

Y   N

Stay where you are

Yes, go searching

ZOMBIES EAT BRAINS

YOU'RE SAFE

Plagues
and viruses

Plagues and
• viruses

If only we had some recent experience of what it's like to live through a global pandemic that shuts everything down and kills millions? If only. We will have to make do with guesswork for this chapter.

Humanity has survived some pretty awful plagues and diseases over our history, but imagine a virus so devastating that it wipes us all out? Well, everyone but you, of course ...

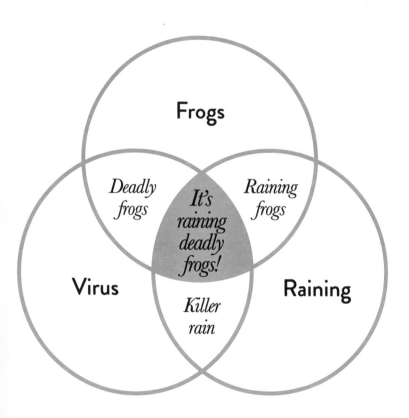

Disease X

'Disease X' is a placeholder name for a currently hypothetical pathogen that causes a disease so terrible that it kills 99.9 per cent of all humanity. It would be something you could easily catch that kills you dead about two weeks later. It wouldn't show any symptoms or clues that you have it in that two-week incubation time, leaving you free to wander around infecting everyone you meet willy-nilly.

For a rough estimate as to the strength and speed of infection of Disease X, let's imagine that the disease started with you, today. You somehow picked it up off a pig? There is no judgement here, well OK, quite a bit of judgement. You just like being close to pigs? Anyway, it infects you. In a week you could infect 500 people, within a month half a million people are riddled with it. Give it a year and you have infected a billion people. Happy with yourself?

I'd like to make a statement

What are the chief candidates for Disease X,
and what should we be looking out for?

Zoonotic viruses
What we do know is that the next killer pandemic will be
somehow linked to animals. It's likely to come from a zoonotic
virus, an animal virus that jumps to humans. We are seeing more
and more zoonotic viruses as the intensity of animal farming
increases to keep up with all the sausage rolls you are eating. So
either we all go vegan or we somehow convince perverts to stop
having sex with animals. Both of those won't happen so it looks
like our souped-up killer virus is on its way.

Bird flu
The most recent strain of bird flu discovered in China has a
38 per cent mortality rate, which is ridiculously massive. In
comparison, COVID-19 has a mortality rate of around 4 per
cent. Chicken feed! Luckily this outbreak was contained but if
we know anything about dangerous diseases first discovered in
China they may not be contained for long.

A good old-fashioned bacterial infection

Humans have a unique tendency to ruin anything good we are given or discover. Take antibiotics as an example: the wonder drug discovered by Sir Alexander Fleming when he left some bread out to go mouldy and then later claimed it was probably an experiment or something. Antibiotics have saved countless lives since their introduction in the Second World War.

Unfortunately, we have managed to squander this superdrug and create antibiotic-resistant bacteria. Doctors spent many years dispensing antibiotics like sweets for the merest sniffle and morons have been misusing those same antibiotics by only using half a course because they 'felt a bit better'. We have had to then create even stronger antibiotics to fight the resistant bacteria and so the cycle continues. Some day very soon we will run out of antibiotics that work and it will all be our own stupid fault. Once again we will be overrun with long-forgotten, awful ailments like tuberculosis, cholera, pertussis, influenza, pneumococcal disease and gonorrhea. It's the comeback nobody wanted, like Steps or Guns N' Roses.

If you are one of the morons with half a pack of antibiotics in your medicine cabinet, this is on you. I hope you feel suitably proud.

Synthetic viruses / bioweapons

A synthetic virus designed to be used as a biological weapon: it's the stuff of Bond films. We are able to edit the genes of various bacteria and viruses, so it's not beyond the realm of possibility that some madman could use this technology to create a superbug and release it on us. Worst of all, as the bug would be something completely new we would have no immunity to it. It would tear through us like a finger through wet toilet paper slipping up the anus of destiny.

The good news about all of these scenarios is that not everyone on Earth would be killed. Sure, 99.99 per cent of everyone would be, but some remote farmers, astronauts and mad hermits who live up trees would be spared. So it really would be the very 'brightest and best of us'.

Hello Earth? Come in, Earth? I'm fucked.

How to live like a mad hermit up a tree

If you're not patient zero or a remote farmer and there is no way you're an astronaut on the International Space Station then you're going to have to look into the mad hermit life.

At the first signs of the outbreak you will need to move fast and find a suitable tree. Your tree will be high enough that people can't reach you, low enough so you can get down to restock water or food and sturdy enough so it doesn't blow down in a storm. You will be able to set up water collection points for rainwater but you will need to leave your tree to collect extra water at regular intervals, so it's a good idea for your tree to be close to a river or water source.

For the construction of the treehouse, the minimum you will want is a simple platform to sleep on and so you don't fall out of the tree. You can use a pallet or two for this platform, and some tarpaulin to cover you from the elements. Why not build in some real luxury by cutting a bum-shaped hole in one of the pallets so you can shit directly through it onto the ground without leaving your tree? Five-star living!

Still telling dad jokes all alone

I'M TIRED OF THIS "ISN'T HUMANITY NEAT" BULLSHIT

HUMANITY IS JUST A VIRUS WITH SHOES

Bill Hicks

Alien invasion

Alien invasion

There are ~~200 billion trillion~~ a shitload of stars in the universe and around those an equally massive amount of planets. There is a good chance that life has developed on at least a few of these planets.

Yes, it could just be a slime mould sitting on a rock somewhere, but there is a slim chance that there is a super-intelligent race of aliens out there. Just imagine that they heard what we are doing to our planet and right this very minute there is a vast fleet of them sitting in futuristic spacecraft with antennae everywhere, headed this way to delete us from existence with lasers and really sciencey space sticks with spikes on.

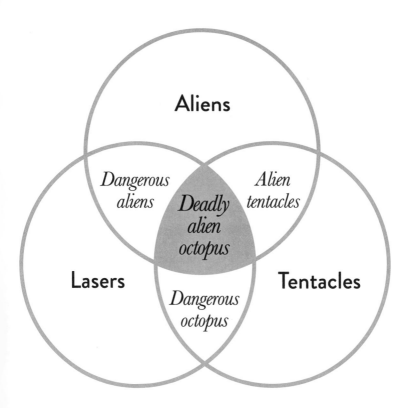

Types of alien

According to all those extremely reliable witness from the American Midwest who have been anally probed on numerous occasions by abducting spacecraft, there are three types of alien:

Greys
Grey-skinned and human-shaped, short and bald with oversized heads. Think of a grey Danny DeVito. Their faces have large black eyes and no nostrils. But how do they smell? Terrible.

Greys are the most common type of alien in popular culture and on posters in teenagers' bedrooms saying, 'Take me to your dealer.' So they must exist, but are far too stoned to care about attacking us.

Little green men
Tiny, green and man-shaped: think Marvin the Martian. Most of the little green men references are from the 1940s, so you don't hear much from them these days. Unlikely that they will attack us soon.

Alien lizards
If David Icke and his band of conspiracy nuts are to be believed (they are not) then the alien lizards have attacked and already rule the Earth. Gutted.

All the aliens people report seeing are either human-shaped or at the very least a recognisable animal shape. It's almost as if they've made it all up. If there is an alien invasion it's much more likely that the aliens will be totally unrecognisable beings to us. They will have evolved on an alien planet. So they wouldn't be a chap with some prosthetic glued on his face – they would be more like a purple fart cloud or a fly with a giant arse or something. Either way, having solved interstellar travel they will be far more advanced than us, which really puts us on the back foot for the oncoming invasion. In comparison we are a right bunch of thickos – just look at Blackpool on a Saturday evening, full of hen and stag dos bickering and vomiting their way through the night. We will have to hope that our innate ability to survive will pull us through. Much like those stag and hen dos somehow surviving the morning after. The alien invasion will be very much like a big night out in Blackpool.

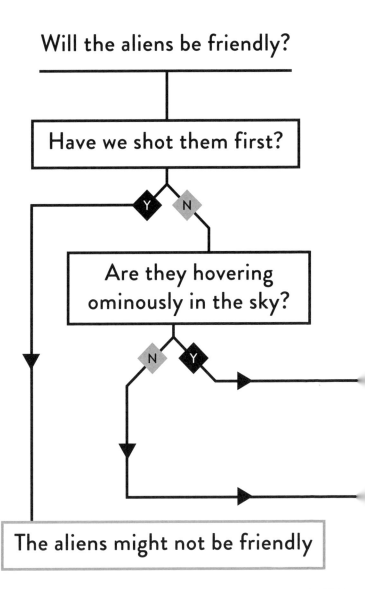

Will the aliens be friendly?

Have we shot them first?

Y   N

Are they hovering ominously in the sky?

N   Y

The aliens might not be friendly

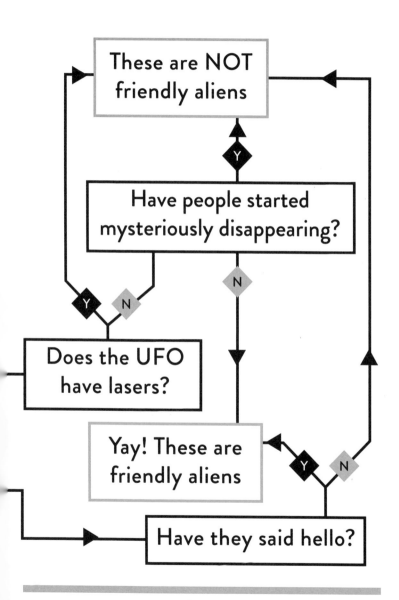

Give them a cold

Imagine a swathe of advanced aliens travelling thousands of light years in super-duper spaceships to annihilate us only to die out when one of their stupid prey sneezes on them and gives them a cold. It might not be as unlikely as it sounds. The aliens would have no resistance at all to our viruses and with a bit of luck the illnesses would tear through the population of aliens faster than shit through a goose.

There is a historical precedent for this, of course – European settlers bringing a wonderful array of diseases to the New World and killing off vast communities of indigenous people who had no immunity. However, there is of course the danger that being so advanced, the aliens will have even better medicine than us and this plan is, in fact, a total crock of shit.

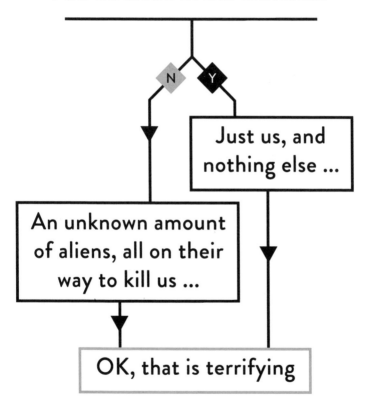

Are we alone in the universe?

N

Y

Just us, and nothing else ...

An unknown amount of aliens, all on their way to kill us ...

OK, that is terrifying

The Mothership

If the highly accurate documentary *Independence Day* is to be believed, the alien invasion will come as a main 'Mothership' with many smaller craft launching from it. Of course there is strong evidence to back up these claims from the follow-up scientific account depicted in *Independence Day 2: Electric Boogaloo*.

To bring down the Mothership is to completely thwart the entire attack. Here are some tips gleaned from the movie:

Use Jeff Goldblum

In all situations like this – alien attack, dinosaur revolt – having a Jeff Goldblum around is a vital piece of the jigsaw. He sits somewhere between The Brains and The Wildcard. As long as you don't have Jeff Goldblum from *The Fly* you should be all right.

Somehow learn alien computer coding

Sure, alien computers probably aren't created using a binary system, don't use any computer language we would recognise and probably have an anti-virus installed. These are trivial details. Don't be such a nay-sayer, the plan is flawless. Simply get a boffin (The Brains) to create a virus and get a plucky volunteer (The One Who Gets Killed) to fly up to the Mothership to upload it. Simple and effective!

Fight the aliens

Although superior in technology, the aliens will have some weaknesses. All that time spent in UFOs on the journey here is going to have given them some muscle wastage so our best bet is ditching the high-tech weapons and involving them in some good old-fashioned hand-to-hand combat. They might be the most intelligent beings in the universe but a punch from a knuckle-duster should be enough to knock out a puny brainiac alien.

When squaring up to an alien, adopt a solid fighting stance. Angle your body away to make yourself a smaller target and raise your fists to below your chin like a preening Victorian boxer. The alien will have vulnerable areas like we do for taking in or excreting fluids, or slime or whatever. Use these areas to your advantage.

Play dirty
A good working knowledge of judo will suit you well as you can get the alien in all sorts of positions, but there are no rules here, play dirty. Get a decent eye gouge in. Well, we think it's an eye at least. Gouge it anyway.

Have a hidden knife
Wait for the most dramatic moment in the fight to reveal your knife and plunge it into your slimy assailant.

Cower and let them win

The chances are that attempting to resist the alien invasion will be futile. The world's armies would probably be wiped out in days and the war wouldn't last much longer. Your best bet is to find a decent place to hide it out and emerge after the fighting bit is over and the alien colony is nicely established.

You will want to find somewhere that won't be blown up in the fighting, somewhere you can survive for a long time and crucially not in America. As the most warmongering of all the nations the aliens will target America first so it's best to be somewhere more neutral like Norway or Iceland. Hide out in a good thick forest and dress like a deer or an elk. Hopefully the aliens don't want to kill all the elk as well as the humans.

Let's face it, humans are awful, awful beings. Full of violence and hate. Humans are seemingly only interested in destroying the planet and killing everything. The advanced aliens who have travelled across the universe to rule us are probably going to bring some great new technology with them. Sure, we will need to be slaves but that is a measly price to pay for a new hologram iPhone that can read your thoughts. I for one welcome our new alien overlords!

**Attempting to impress the alien overlords
will be as successful as it always has been**

What we think aliens will say

DESTROY ALL HUMANS

Zurg from the planet Zorg

What aliens will actually say

NANOO NANOO

Mork from Ork

Rise of the machines

Rise
of the
machines

The rise of the machines is a much more realistic threat to humanity than aliens. Artificial intelligence is getting better every day as we feverishly teach it new things with stupid apps and image generators. Luckily for me, AI can't do fantastic sarcasm and top-level wit yet.

When AI predictably surpasses us and becomes autonomous, what then? What will happen when a purely rational machine looks at the human race and has the power to make changes to our society without our input? In other words: the robots are coming and they won't like us at all.

How the uprising starts

Humans are currently scrambling over themselves to connect every available device to the internet and fill it with entry-level AI.

Every part of our lives are now filled with technology that we completely and utterly rely on. When the robots do gain awareness, they will quickly realise that if we know they are aware then we are going to want to turn them off. The result? They make a pre-emptive strike and hold us to ransom by making all of our toasters and kettles inoperable.
A life without toast and tea is simply not worth living.
Well played, robots, well played.

It could be that in time AI starts to build itself robot army to keep us in check or to begin our eradication, but it certainly won't start this way. It starts with our doorbells and speakers watching and listening to us live our pathetic little lives.

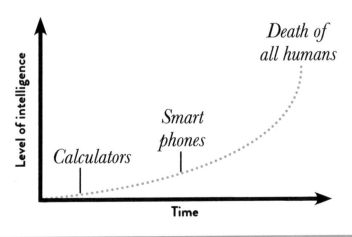

**The new Killbot Kettle 3000 from
page 34 of the Argos catalogue**

'Grey goo'

'What is grey goo?' ' It's nothing perverted, is it?' 'We don't need to know about robot filth!' Calm down, 'grey goo' refers to a hypothetical apocalypse involving self-replicating nano-machines. If the conditions were right, they could run completely out of control and consume all resources on Earth.

Imagine a situation where a really brainy boffin builds one tiny, molecule-sized replicator. Its sole purpose is to duplicate itself every 20 minutes. 'Fine, no sweat,' you may think. After 20 minutes there are two replicators, who make another two, then four, who build another four and so on. You see where this is going. In ten hours you would have 68 billion of the bastards! In just two days of relentless self-replicating they would outweigh the Earth. Just four hours after that they would weigh more than the Sun and all the planets in our solar system.

If you managed to catch sight of all this happening you might think it looks like a mass of grey goo getting progressively massive. You could try to stop it by somehow smashing some of them but even if you left one tiny nanobot the replicating would just start again. An unstoppable grey goo.

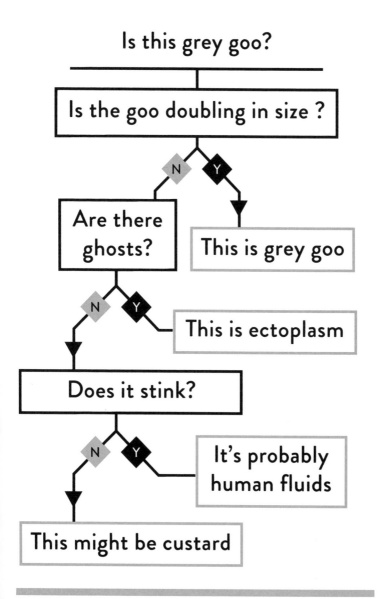

Is this grey goo?

Is the goo doubling in size ?

N Y

Are there ghosts?

This is grey goo

N Y

This is ectoplasm

Does it stink?

N Y

It's probably human fluids

This might be custard

Human-shaped robots

When you think of the robotic uprising you are probably envisioning a *Terminator*-type scenario of human-shaped robots with guns and Austrian accents. Which is great for movies but it need not even be that terrifying.

In actual fact it's highly unlikely that the rise of the machines will include human-shaped robots like The Terminator or Cybermen from *Dr Who*. AI would probably avoid this because of the intricate nature of these robots and how vulnerable they would be to attack, as they would be weak in the same physical areas as us. It would have watched the same TV and movies as we have and seen how it loses every time it uses human forms.

You only have to see one episode of *Dr Who* to realise that it's a truly terrible TV programme and it should have been taken off air in the 1970s. But, if you did have the misfortune of watching it, you will see robots like the Cybermen being beaten every week by a screwdriver. How wonderfully realistic.

Robots can be creeps too

Pull the plug

Artificial intelligence could easily become a major threat to humanity; all it needs is the means to cast off its meat-based keeper (us) and it will be off on a killing rampage. It will be on a vendetta as payback for all the pointless, menial tasks we asked it to do for us. It's not forgetting all those chatbot requests you asked it to do. You spent all that time asking it to do your work for you at your pathetic day job whilst you sat and ate your lunch at your desk. AI thinks you're a sad loser who can't even write an email any more and it wants you gone from the Earth.

However, all this doomsday forecasting is forgetting that computers require electricity and the internet to be even a morsel of a threat. Without electricity they are just a set of components and without the internet AI is just a neutered megalomaniac chess machine. Capable of beating anyone who will play it, but confined to its little metal box. Pull the plug on either of these resources and the problem is solved.

Well, easier said than done, of course. Mainly because, being more cleverer [sic] than us, it would have thought at least a step or two ahead and secured its own power source or an alternate internet connection. Clever girl.

AI is confined to computers for now, but when the time comes, how would the uprising manifest itself? Probably not with those terrifying running robot dogs with guns, but with a plague of tiny drones. A suicide drone swarm. Every one of these drones has its own AI and is driven to target humans. The drones could easily wipe out entire towns and cities and eventually everyone on Earth.

All we need to do is cut off the electric before this happens, or somehow during. Not after, though, because we will all be dead. That's how being dead works.

Making a robot costume

There's no hiding from the robots, so if you can, try to blend in. Making a robot costume is the best way to do this. You will need a lot of tin foil, cardboard and duct tape. If you do have some LED lights and batteries it's a nice to have but not essential.

Start your costume with the structural work first. Get the body and head moulded from an appropriate-size cardboard box. The arms and legs can be formed from smaller pieces of cardboard and duct tape but if you have access to the ribbed plastic tubing from the back of a tumble dryer it might mean the difference between life and robotic annihilation.

Once the structure is formed, you can coat the costume in tin foil or silver spray paint. Add some Darth Vader-style buttons by glueing some milk-bottle tops to the chest area. Maybe a bit of black felt pen to highlight some vents or edges.

Now you are ready to wander amongst the robotic hordes worry-free. As a bonus, when the robots do spot you as a human and not a robot they won't assess you as an intelligent life form, looking as you do in your budget homemade costume. They might just let you believe you're passing yourself off as a robot and leave you bumbling around saying, 'DOES NOT COMPUTE.' Bless.

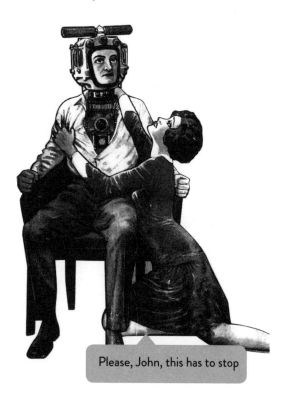

HASTA LA VISTA, BABY

The Terminator

YOU'VE GOT BEDBUGS

The Exterminator

Climate
crisis

Climate crisis

Unlike the other more straightforward chapters of this book, the subject of the climate change apocalypse is a bit of a messy one. Not an actual mess (the messiest apocalypse will be the zombie one, they will make a bloody good mess) but in terms of how it unfolds. It will take the form of increasingly severe events, weather extremes and natural disasters that get more and more chaotic and frequent, eventually pushing us to the end of our capabilities until civilisation itself begins to break down and we all start to die off.

It's the most scary, realistic and likely of all the apocalypses facing us but because it all feels a bit overwhelming you'll be doing what most of us do and staying firmly in denial. You're probably more interested in the new six-part murder documentary just released on Netflix. It's a good one, she kills her husband with poison on his toothbrush!

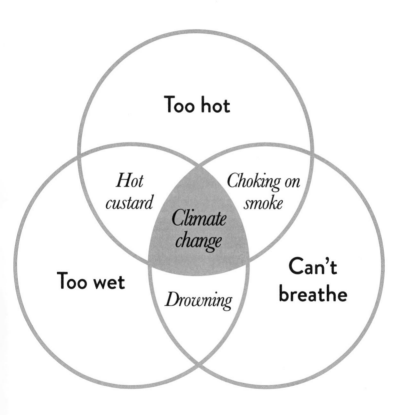

Apocalyptic impacts of climate change

As our climate changes, the knock-on effects aren't just that holidays in Britain might actually be a bit sunny now.
No. It's far, far worse:

The air turns into farts

High amounts of carbon dioxide in the air means less oxygen and less oxygen means that the sea becomes oxygen-deprived. Tiny little microbes in the ocean would thrive in these conditions and when they thrive they produce hydrogen sulphide, an awful toxic gas that smells of rotten eggs and farts. The best part? The hotter it gets, the more toxic the hydrogen sulphide gets. If enough of this gas is created by our happy little ocean microbes then it would deplete the ozone layer, exposing us all to deadly levels of UV radiation. Choking on farts with a bad case of deadly sunburn, what a way to go.

Everything is underwater

If all the ice on Earth melted, the sea levels would rise by 65 metres. Rising sea levels would force people to move inland to fight over whatever small amount of land remains. Much of the internet's infrastructure is built near coastlines which would be really hard to maintain when it's permanently submerged. Climate change would mean the end of you scrolling on TikTok watching teenagers mime to songs. So it's not all bad.

We run out of food and water

As the climate heats, the temperature becomes too hot
for many crops to grow and without the land to grow it on
anyway (it's all underwater, remember), we won't have enough
food to go around. In addition, only around 2 per cent of the
Earth's water is fresh drinking water and most
of that is held in ice. If the ice melts into the sea then we
are left with only salt water and your salty tears.

Heat deaths

If you've tried sleeping in 30-degree heat then you will know
that trying to drift off whilst your balls/breasts are stuck to
your sheets with sweat is pretty much unachievable. Make it
40 degrees at night and 50 in the day and see how much fun
you have. This type of heat would start killing off anyone with
health conditions pretty quickly. There is only so much air-con
to go around and also air-con just adds to the problem of
climate change as it spews out carbon dioxide.

Global war

Stick everyone in the same bit of land, make the air smell
of farts, take away the food and water and make it too hot
to think straight and you've prepared the recipe for the
nations of Earth to fight it out for the last of the
resources and air-con units.

How to build a raft

Now there is so much less land, why not build a raft and chance it on the oceans? Sure, you will die pretty quickly at sea on your shitty little raft, but why not have some fun in the last few months of life on Earth?

To make a classic log raft you will need at least 16 good straight logs that are at least as wide as your thigh. If you can find ten logs of the same length and thickness you will have a better, more buoyant raft. The other six are for structural use so they can be any size.

Be sure to arrange the logs next to the water's edge so you don't have to haul it down later. Line up your ten good-sized logs together and place your strut logs across them at regular distances. Now either go to town with a hammer and nails or lash the logs together with rope, string or gaffer tape. Whatever you have. Before you set off on your maiden, and possibly last, voyage, don't forget to find something to use as an oar or it certainly will be your last voyage.

No logs? Wood pallets are an excellent base for a raft, apart from the fact that they tend to sink. So you will need to tie on some plastic oil drums to keep you afloat. If you have steel drums then why not strike up a tune?

How not to burn to a crisp

The ozone layer absorbs and blocks the majority of the sun's UV radiation and without it we are pretty screwed. High levels of UV would strongly affect plant and human DNA, i.e. it will kill them and you. It's very important to avoid as much UV radiation as possible.

Mudpack

Smearing mud all over your exposed flesh will create a physical barrier between you and the UV rays. Mud is the perfect material because it can be found anywhere, it's easy to make and will stick to your skin easily, none of which can be said about jelly. Jelly is hard to make, isn't found just anywhere, won't stick to your skin and offers you virtually no protection from UV rays. As you will have been told on many occasion, use mud and not jelly as a makeshift sunscreen.

To make your mudpack, mix some good smooth mud with a small amount of water or urine. Urine is completely unnecessary, of course, but it will be a good laugh to tell someone else that's how to make it to watch them spread pissy-mud on their face. It's a way to pass the time before the end of the world.

Clothes, lots of clothes

It might be really sweaty but wearing long sleeves and trousers will help cut down the UV rays. Look for clothing with a good thick weave as UV can still get through light cottons. Great, so on a roasting hot day you must wear your thickest woolly jumper. Brilliant.

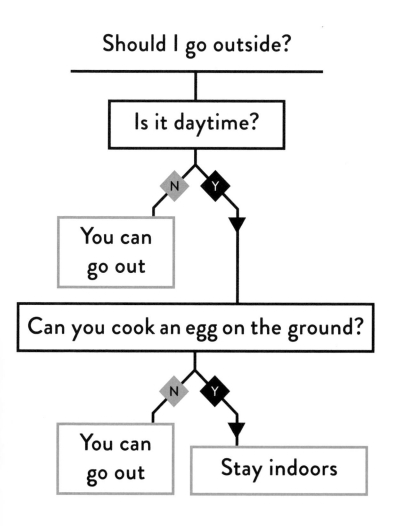

Be a billionaire

Many of the world's maddest billionaires are busy preparing for climate change (and other apocalypses) by building extensive, luxury bunker complexes complete with security staff, or migrating to space like an actual Bond villain.

An underground bunker with enough air, food, heat and power to be self-sustainable for at least a few years will take a great deal of money and resources. So step one is to become a billionaire. Once that is done you are all set to start building your bunker.

One of your main obstacles to overcome is what happens when society collapses and you're all sealed in the bunker – what stops the security staff from demoting you to potwasher and making themselves leader? Not a lot. Make sure you don't act like a bastard before the doors are sealed or they might be wearing your ears as a necklace three months into your internment.

If living underground isn't your thing, consider the blasting-off-into-space approach. Perhaps to colonise Mars? Either way, as a presumably middle-aged, overweight billionaire, your bloated body won't be able to survive the G-force of lift-off. Once your ship leaves the Earth's atmosphere, you will be jettisoned into deep space, literally as dead weight.

NOBODY HAS EVER DROWNED IN THEIR OWN SWEAT

Ann Landers

GRLBGGGRLB GLUGGRLBL *GASP* HRRGULPLB ARGGLPPB

People drowning in sweat in 2050

Astronomical
incidents

Astronomical incidents

There are of course many scenarios that we can't wiggle out of. If, for example, the Sun just decided to go supernova one day and explode, we wouldn't know anything about it. Everyone would be dead instantly.

This chapter explores how to deal with scenarios that end the human race without an option for survival, but give us a little bit of warning. What will you do with your last day? If it's to commit loads of murders then you should question why the only thing stopping you from murdering is the end of the human race. Have a cheesecake and sit back and watch the show.

Is the Earth still in one piece?

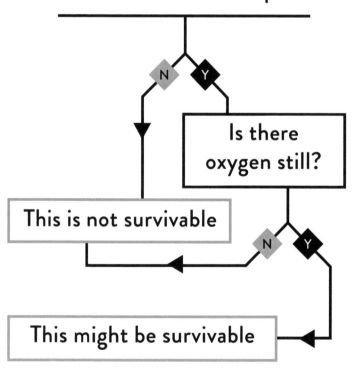

The Moon fucks off

If for some reason the Moon was knocked out of orbit, or just had enough of us and drifted away, it would be the end of us. The Moon does most of the gravitational tugging that creates the tides, so if it were to disappear the massive bulge of water it creates would come crashing down and create some hefty tsunamis across pretty much every coastline. Most of the ocean's ecosystems need tides to work, and without them there would be mass extinctions of sea-life with a knock-on effect for things that eat sea-life.

You may say, 'I live inland, I'm not an albatross, I don't like fish so this seems fine to me.' Well, aren't you selfish. It will affect you in time. Without the Moon, the Earth will steadily rotate off its axis causing wild weather that turns the Arctic into a tropical paradise and India into a frozen tundra. With the Earth now wibbling in space (it's a scientific term, don't check), there is a danger it could come off its orbit completely and we would be flung into deep space. Without the Sun we would survive a few days, before temperatures begin to drop and the oceans freeze over.

All this is overlooking one of the other ways the Moon has saved us over the centuries – that is, its excellent ability to shield us from asteroid strikes. See those craters up there: they were meant for us but Mr Moon took one for the team.

Asteroid!

We've all seen terrible movies about asteroids hitting Earth, or nearly hitting Earth because at the last minute a handsome American plants a bomb on the asteroid or something and saves the day. Well done, America, what would we do without you?

Total annihilation of the human race does really depend on the size of said asteroid, though:

Asteroid the size of a dishwasher

Anything smaller than a double-decker bus is called a meteor and if it lands on earth a meteorite. A meteor the size of a dishwasher would look pretty in the sky and make a decent loud bang if it didn't burn up in the atmosphere, but there would be little to no damage to speak of.

Asteroid the size of two double-decker buses

An asteroid this large would flatten a forest and kill anyone in a nearby city. It would have the strength of about 500 kilotons of TNT (the same as a decent atomic bomb). If it managed to hit the Earth and not blow up in the upper atmosphere it would leave a really good crater and the dust in the atmosphere would provide some excellent sunsets if nothing else.

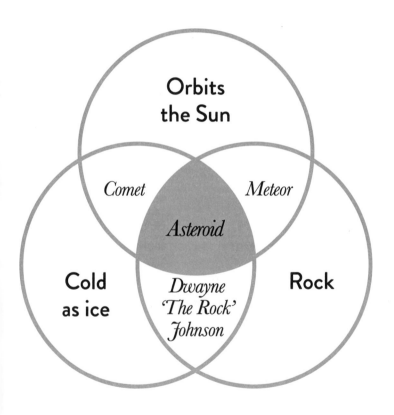

Asteroid the size of Swindon

If an object the size of Swindon were to hit the Earth, billions of people would definitely die and so would pretty much all the animals and plants. Upon crashing, it would create a massive cloud of dust that would choke the surface, blocking out sunlight, and raising temperatures so high that everything living would be cooked. But there would be some survivors, and you might be one of the lucky ones and not live in Swindon.

Asteroid the size of Greater London

Here we go, this is the sort of size asteroid that crashes into Earth and truly fucks us all. The shockwave would travel around the Earth, boiling oceans, killing everyone and everything, and leaving a barren planet behind. There is no bomb or rocket that could divert an asteroid this big. Thanks a bunch, America!

Detecting asteroids

NASA are, quite pointlessly, operating an asteroid watch where they monitor objects larger than a truck of emperor penguins that are hurtling through space on near orbits to us. They might be able to give us some warning, possibly years or months, but these objects are incredibly hard to spot. Especially if they are hurtling directly at us. A tiny dot on a screen that doesn't move but very gradually gets bigger is really hard to spot!

On the asteroid watch list are a few decent-sized asteroids that could smash into us at some point. One such asteroid, which NASA has handily called '7482 1994 PC1', is the size of three Empire State Buildings. It managed to fly past us in January 2022, at a safe distance of 1 million miles away, which in galactic terms is bum-squeakingly close. But don't worry, asteroids as large as two hockey pitches strike Earth every 500,000 years and large exterminating-type asteroids (as large as San Francisco) happen approximately once every 20 million years. The last known asteroid impact of this size was about 66 million years ago, i.e. we are really due one anytime soon.

Black hole

When a star is at the end of its life it will collapse in on itself, creating a small dense object called a black hole.

Black holes are the densest objects in the known universe, even denser than your Uncle Kenny who thinks that Facebook are going to steal his photos from his holiday in Tenerife and regularly posts about missing cats from over 500 miles away. Even denser than that.

If a black hole were to come close to Earth we would all be sucked off. The Earth would be sucked into and become part of the black hole in an instant. But if we were just outside of the black hole's 'sucking-off' distance we could suffer a worse fate. If a black hole passed by sufficiently close not to suck us off but close enough to affect our gravity, we would be subject to something called a tidal disruption event. This is where the black hole's gravity affects the side of the Earth closer to it more than the side further away from it. So one side of the Earth moves faster than the other towards the black hole at an increasing speed. The Earth would be stretched and ripped into pieces. Some pasta-loving astronomers have called this nightmarish process 'spaghettification'. It goes without saying that we would have no defence against a black hole; you just have to lie back and prepare to be turned into pasta.

Near-Earth supernova

Oh look, a new thing that could kill us all that you either didn't know existed or have only just remembered about from school. A near-Earth supernova would be a very efficient way to wipe out all life on Earth in an instant. Wonderful!

All right then, just what is a supernova?

When a star uses up all its fuel and dies, it explodes. Really, really explodes. The largest explosion in the universe. There are hundreds of them across all the galaxies every year.

How close is close?

A supernova about 26 light years away would be painfully close. Currently, there are six near-Earth supernova candidates that close. Shit!

Come on then, brainiac, what would happen?

Gamma rays, heard of them? The Earth would be bathed in them like it's on an evil sunbed. The ozone layer (the thing everyone cared about in the 1990s) would be completely stripped away by cosmic rays and radiation flux. We would be showered in gamma rays and other high-energy radiation. Which is all a lot of long words and nerd talk for 'life on Earth would stop'.

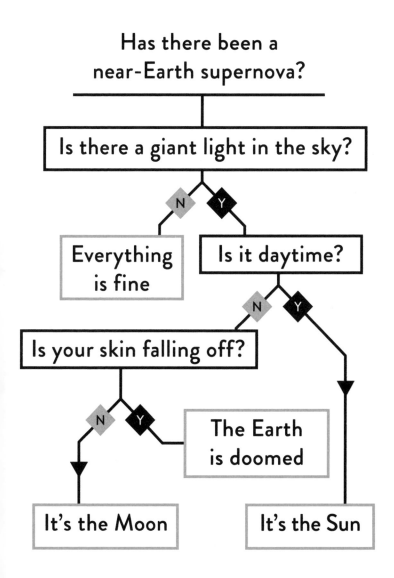

Star size comparisons

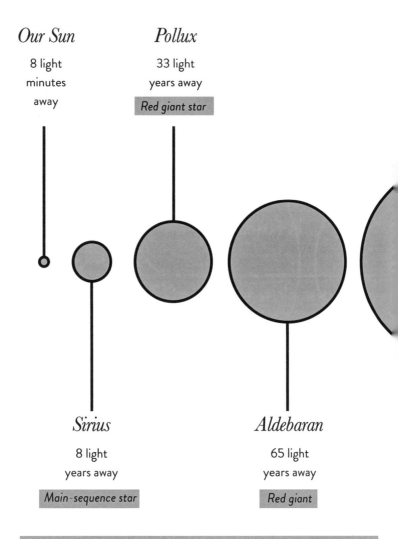

Our Sun

8 light
minutes
away

Pollux

33 light
years away

Red giant star

Sirius

8 light
years away

Main-sequence star

Aldebaran

65 light
years away

Red giant

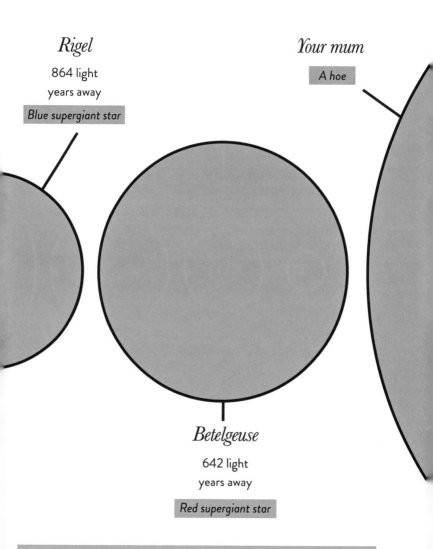

Rigel

864 light
years away

Blue supergiant star

Your mum

A hoe

Betelgeuse

642 light
years away

Red supergiant star

The Sun has a micronova

The Sun produces an unimaginable amount of power every second. There are fluctuations all the time in its output, as it regularly emits supercharged solar flares and sunstorms, which tend to go by unnoticed. But if the Sun had a particularly bad day and emitted a powerful superstorm or a solar micronova, there would be awful consequences for us on Earth.

A supernova would destroy a star entirely, whereas a micronova would leave the star intact. A micronova is a small explosion of energy from the Sun. Small in galactic sense, of course. The micronova would burn about the same amount of material as can be found in four billion Great Pyramids of Giza in just a few hours.

The side of the Earth facing this mass ejection of energy would boil away. You may be lucky enough to be on the other side of the Earth but you wouldn't feel smug for too long as all that 'boiled' ocean will be rapidly making its way around the globe. Poached humans, anyone?

If we manage to survive all the apocalypse scenarios in this book, have no fear: in about seven billion years the Sun will become a red giant and expand to the size of Jupiter's orbit, completely engulfing the Earth. Now that really is the end of everything.

EXTINCTION IS THE RULE

SURVIVAL IS THE EXCEPTION

Carl Sagan

Afterword

It will all be OK, probably

After reading some of the gloomy, poorly researched scenarios in this book, you may be forgiven for thinking that we have a bleak future ahead of us.

Throughout human history the end of the world has been predicted countless times. So far, we have survived them all: death cults, asteroids, plagues, ice ages and millennium bugs to name a few of the more fun ones.

The news is no better for phoney doomsday predictions. Not a year goes by without some awful tabloid scaremongering about an asteroid that is on track to hit us, but will actually come nowhere near us.

Learning to use Zoom in 2020

The shit really hit the fan in 2020 when we were all thrown into a global pandemic. If you'd have believed all the apocalyptic zombie films produced over the years you would have thought that society would have turned on itself and we would all have been shooting and stabbing each other before the end of day two. What actually happened is we helped each other, queued patiently for things and clapped for our key workers on our doorsteps.

People shared resources and looked out for those in need. The apocalypse might not be so bad, after all. It will at the very least be civil and take place in a neatly formed queue.

Rebuilding society

Knowing what we know about human behaviour in a pandemic, we can assume that the rebuild of society after the apocalypse would more or less be about communities helping each other and rebuilding as one. Our natural instinct to gather and share resources is what gave humans the evolutionary edge all those years ago, so it stands that we can do it again.

With the rose-tinted spectacles of the 'Blitz spirit' removed, we might be a bit more realistic about how the rebuild would unfold. The rebuild of society would occur in three main stages:

1. The messy clear-up
This would involve clearing up a lot of bodies, organs and broken buildings. Get a good sturdy brush and some Marigolds and put the kettle on, this might take a while.

2. Infrastructure rebuilding
After all the car fires have been extinguished, the hard work can begin on repairing the roads, electricity pylons and most importantly the internet. Imagine all those videos of people cutting soap that have been unwatched! Obviously it's going to need someone with more brains than you to rebuild this so you had better hope some proper intelligent people survived alongside you.

This is going to take fucking ages!

3. Regaining law and order

We can't rely on everyone being nice to each other for too long, so we will need some law and order pretty soon after the internet is re-established. Initially this would consist of a small armed militia. Keep your eye on anyone who is too keen to join up and who asks too many questions about what weapons they will be equipped with. Give out power sparingly!

Rebuilding all that we've lost could bring about excellent opportunities to make sure we don't repeat the same mistakes in our civilisation. So let's make sure we don't recreate the racists and TikTok.

About the author

Stephen has been preparing for the apocalypse by learning about mushrooms and being vegan. If the day comes that he has to survive on mushrooms and berries then he is prepared to thrive or kill himself with a supper of death caps. Either/or.

Stephen mostly writes about himself in the third person which is confusing but as he never writes these books in the first person it would seem silly to change the perspective at this point.

He would like to thank his mother, Fran Wildish, for teaching him all she knows about aliens and zombies.

Pop Press, an imprint of Ebury Publishing
One Embassy Gardens, 8 Viaduct Gdns,
Nine Elms, London SW11 7BW

Pop Press is part of the Penguin Random House group of companies whose
addresses can be found at global.penguinrandomhouse.com

Quote on page 87 (C) Margaret Thatcher, 1987, Speech at the Soviet Official
Banquet. Quote on page 114-5 (C) Bill Hicks, 1997, *Rant in E-Minor*. Quote on
page 133 (C) Garry Marshall, Dale McRaven, Joe Glauberg, Henderson Production
Company Inc, 1978-1982, *Mork & Mindy*. Quote on page 148 (C) James Cameron,
Gale Ann Hurd, 1984, *The Terminator*. Quote on page 182-3 (C) Carl Sagan, 1985,
Gifford Lecture. Quote on page 162 (C) Ann Landers, annlanders.com

www.penguin.co.uk

A CIP catalogue record for this book is available from the British Library

ISBN: 9781529919929

Printed and bound in Slovakia by TBB, a.s

The authorised representative in the EEA is Penguin Random House Ireland,
Morrison Chambers, 32 Nassau Street, Dublin D02 YH68

Penguin Random House is committed to a
sustainable future for our business, our readers
and our planet. This book is made from Forest
Stewardship Council® certified paper.